# THE
# VILLA HOLIDAY
# COOKBOOK

## BY

Tony Nelson

Published by
A & P Nelson & Company
Ascotts
Felbridge
West Sussex RH19 2PS
www.villaholidaycookbook.com

First published 2009

© 2009 Anthony N Nelson

ISBN 978-0-9561859-0-7

Cover photographs by Bran Symondson

This book is a collection of mouth-watering recipes
and practical tips designed for
self-catering holidays.

The recipes have been carefully selected to cater for a
range of tastes with the minimum effort – you are on
holiday after all - and without using a large array of pots,
pans, utensils and cooking facilities– but with some great
flavours and textures and healthy Mediterranean style
ingredients.

Although originally developed for villa or apartment
holidays around the Mediterranean, most of the
ingredients can be found in good UK supermarkets and
so the recipes are also fine at home.

The recipes have been written in a clear, step by step,
way which the less experienced cook can easily follow.

# CONTENTS

# CHAPTER 1

## INTRODUCTION

I have always enjoyed my food. Especially the southern European variety which goes so well with the lazy, hazy days of a summer holiday. I also enjoy self-catering because of the freedom, cost-saving, relaxation and range of choice. And I enjoy putting meals together. So whenever our family goes on a self-catering holiday I always insist that I will do all the cooking and my wife mustn't lift a finger.

There are several good reasons for this:

- I can tear myself away from the pool at beer o'clock and help myself to something cool from the fridge while I throw lunch together
- The family do the washing-up
- My wife is impressed and enjoys telling her friends that I always do all the cooking when we go on holiday.
- The yummy mummies then look on me with warm approval and give their partners a hard time because they don't do the same.
- It is a lot less expensive than eating out and the food is less boring than a set meal in a hotel package
- No-one has to dress up for it

Of course I like eating out too and try to alternate a meal out with one in or a picnic.

It is a game for me that at the end of the holiday I leave as little left-over food as possible. This a real challenge to invent unusual combinations of food in the last few days of a holiday (hence the fried peas and some of the other recipes, although the soused cucumber in gin ended up on the cutting-room floor).

## RELAX AND ENJOY

You've had a long stressful day getting to your villa or apartment, the early start, the airport, the flight, the drive, change of climate, finding the place, unpacking.........you may not feel like going out to eat and you certainly don't feel up to cooking an elaborate meal (even if you were able to find a shop open and to do the First Shop).

The answer is to take your first meal with you. My personal favourites for this purpose are Spaghetti alla Putanesca or Spaghetti with tomatoes and garlic (both recipes in this book). You can make the sauce a day or two before your holiday and put it in a sturdy jar with a well-fitting lid in the fridge, then pack it, well wrapped, in your hold luggage with a pack of dried spaghetti and a packet of grated parmesan. If you prefer to eat out it will keep, but otherwise all you have to do is cook the spaghetti and reheat the sauce and voila you have a comforting meal in minutes.

# THE FIRST SHOP

All the recipes and shopping lists are based on feeding a family of four.
On holiday we try to buy this set of basics on the way to our accommodation so we can relax knowing we will be self-sufficient for a while and can please ourselves whether to go out or stay in. Once you have this lot you will only need to buy a few additional ingredients to make many of the recipes in this book.

The list looks a bit long and we find its best to photocopy it in advance and give a section to each member of the party or put their initials against the items they can be relied on to find. You can bribe younger kids by letting them add a few treats ( I suggest you limit it to two each otherwise you may have month's supply of ice-cream, fizzy drinks and sweets).

From this list you can produce the following meals from this book. Of course you can buy anything else that takes your fancy or add ingredients for other recipes, but these should keep you going:

- Chicken a la Nicoise
- Potato salad
- Green salad
- Tomato salad with basil or oregano
- Spanish potato omelette (tortilla)
- A hearty Enthusiastic Salad*
- Spaghetti with tomato and garlic sauce
- Spaghetti alla Puttanesca
- Salade Nicoise

The first shop is best done in a supermarket, if there is one open when you arrive, but for later purchases of fresh produce, especially fruit and vegetables, it is usually best to go to the roadside stalls which abound in Europe, specialist shops, or the local market if you can.

* so called because you put everything you've got into it.

**SHOPPING LIST – THE FIRST SHOP**

| DRINKS | FRUIT AND VEG | STAPLES |
|---|---|---|
| WINE | SMALL POTATOES | TEA |
| BEER | FRENCH BEANS | COFFEE |
| BOTTLED WATER | LETTUCE | MILK |
| SOFT DRINKS or JUICES | TOMATOES | HONEY or SUGAR |
| | SPANISH/RED ONIONS | BUTTER |
| | APPLES OR PEARS | BREAD |
| **MEAT** | GARLIC | JAM |
| CHORIZO (preferably the cooking variety) | FRESH BASIL | OLIVE OIL (one bottle of extra virgin for dressings and one of ordinary oil for cooking) |
| BACON | LEMONS | RED WINE VINEGAR |
| 1.5 KG CHICKEN PIECES | ORANGES | DRIED OREGANO |
| PROSCIUTTO | RED PEPPERS | SALT |
| SALAMI/SAUCISSON | | PEPPER |
| | | TIN or JAR OF FLAGEOLET or CANNELINI BEANS or CHICK PEAS |
| | **OTHER** | CHEESE (FETA, GRUYERE or EMMENTHAL) |
| | LOO PAPER | JAR of SUNDRIED TOMTOES |
| | TISSUES | 2 x 350g cans TINNED TOMATOES |
| | MATCHES | 1 JAR BLACK OLIVES |
| | WASHING-UP LIQUID | BREAKFAST CEREALS |
| | WASHING POWDER | SPAGHETTI |
| | BIN BAGS | 12 EGGS |
| | KITCHEN TOWELS | RICE (easy cook long grain) |
| | | 2 JARS OR TINS of TUNA |
| | | 2 TINS ANCHOVY FILLETS |
| | | 1 JAR CAPERS |
| | | CHICKEN STOCK CUBES |
| | | 1 JAR of DIJON MUSTARD |

**ITEMS TO TAKE WITH YOU (or buy with the first shop if you forgot)**

SUNSCREEN
AFTER SUN
INSECT REPELLANT
ANTI-HISTAMINE CREAM (for insect bites)
ANTI-MOSQUITO DEVICES (we use the electrical ones with tablets)
A TORCH
A TRAVEL PLUG (OR TWO)
SWISS ARMY KNIFE ( or separate can opener/bottle opener/corkscrew)
(don't forget to pack these in the checked luggage- they won't be allowed in
carry-on luggage)
STICKING PLASTERS
LARGE RE-USABLE SHOPPING BAGS (not only are you saving the
planet, and money, but they are useful as beach bags)
TEA TOWELS and J-CLOTHS
MATCHES
CLOTHES PEGS

**Items not to forget to take with you:**
**PASSPORTS**
**DRIVING LICENCES**
**CREDIT CARDS (and don't forget to take the telephone numbers to call**
**the credit card company if your card is lost or stolen or if the bank**
**refuses to honour a card payment because you forgot to tell them in**
**advance that you were going abroad.)**
**CURRENCY ( including some coins for the luggage trolleys and car park**
**exits at the airport)**

# LUNCHES

An eating style which works well on holiday is a form of tapas selection which has enough variety to satisfy all tastes and appetites and is dead easy to put together. Especially because continental (and these days many UK) supermarkets have a wonderful variety of items in jars which can be kept in the fridge when opened and reappear on the lunch table until finished
The following store cupboard items can be included:
- Slices of saucisson sec, salami or chorizo
- Parma ham
- Pate
- Olives
- Sundried tomatoes in oil
- Chargrilled artichokes in oil
- Chargrilled peeled red peppers in oil
- Flageolet or cannelini beans from a jar or tin, rinsed in cold water, drained and pepped up by stirring gently into them some French dressing or olive oil which you have previously shaken in a jar with some crushed garlic and/or chilli pepper cut into tiny dice. Of course if the olives or sundried tomatoes came in a similar olive oil mix and you like the taste of it, then use that!

Fresh items which are really easy:
- French bread (baguette) or ciabiatta
- Melon
- Tomato salad - slices of ripe tomato on a plate with torn basil leaves or dried oregano or marjoram, drizzled with olive oil
- Tsatsiki (cucumber in yoghurt – see recipe below)
- Green salad with vinaigrette dressing
- Potato salad (see recipe below)

11

- French beans or asparagus cooked, refreshed under cold water and then tossed with a little vinaigrette dressing
- Fried peas (see recipe below)
- Frittata or Spanish omelette (tortilla) (see recipes below)
- Fresh fruit
- Cheese

For something a little more centred, a combination of some of the above ingredients according to your taste, can be put together in a large bowl or platter to make an Enthusiastic Salad.

For those who like a precise recipe to follow I give one below.

# LUNCH RECIPES
## (these can be made separately or a combination can be made as a tapas meal)

| RECIPE | PAGE |
|---|---|
| Enthusiastic salad | 14 |
| Tomato and bread salad | 16 |
| Couscous | 17 |
| Salade Nicoise | 19 |
| Moules a la creme | 21 |
| Baked aubergine and tomato | 23 |
| Cannelini beans with chorizo | 25 |
| Courgette salad | 26 |
| Rice with chorizo and prawns | 27 |
| Greek salad | 28 |
| Pizza | 29 |
| Fried peas with bacon | 31 |
| Spanish potato omelette (tortilla) | 32 |
| Frittata | 34 |
| Pinarello omelette | 36 |
| Tsatsiki | 38 |
| Hot goats cheese salad | 39 |
| Chorizo in red wine | 40 |

# ENTHUSIASTIC SALAD

**Ingredients (for 4):**
**Lemon vinaigrette dressing:**
3 tablespoons lemon juice
6 tablespoons olive oil
I teaspoon Dijon mustard
I large clove garlic peeled, cut small and crushed to a paste with 1
level teaspoon of salt in a small bowl or cup using the back of a
spoon to do the crushing
Black pepper

12 small salad potatoes, skins on, washed
8 spring onions or a good handful of chives chopped small
200 grams green beans
200g saucisson or chorizo cut into slices and each slice halved
100 grams gruyere or emmenthal cheese cut into dice-sized dice
A handful of olives
12 sundried tomatoes cut in half
1 lettuce (cos, lamb's lettuce, lollo rosso or whatever you prefer)

**Method**
1. wash and dry the lettuce. If you don't have a salad spinner,
   put the washed lettuce in a dry tea towel, make sure you
   have it firmly by the corners, take it outside and then spin
   the towel around your head. If you can sprinkle a sun-bather
   you get an extra 5 points. Line a salad bowl with the salad
   leaves.
2. shake the vinaigrette dressing ingredients vigorously
   together in a screw-top jar
3. place the potatoes in a saucepan of salted cold water, bring
   to the boil and cook until tender (about 12 minutes). When
   cooked, drain in a colander and toss the warm potatoes in the
   vinaigrette dressing in a bowl. Leave to cool.
4. cut the stalks off the beans and place in a saucepan of
   boiling water for 5 minutes until cooked (spear one with a

14

fork after 4 minutes and take a bite to see if it is done). When cooked drain in a colander and "refresh" (i.e. place under a tap of cold running water until cold.). Add to the potatoes with the sundried tomatoes and give them a stir together so the beans get a bit of dressing.

5. place the potatoes, sundried tomatoes and beans in the bowl on top of the lettuce
6. scatter over the olives, gruyere cubes and saucisson
7. serve

# TOMATO and BREAD SALAD

Serves 4 for lunch
Preparation: 20 minutes
**Ingredients**
1 French stick or ciabatta, preferably a day old
3 tablespoons olive oil
4 large ripe tomatoes peeled by plunging into boiling water for 1 minute then slipping off the skins and slicing
1 ripe yellow or red pepper, stalk and core removed de-seeded and very finely sliced (or if you prefer use cooked and cooled green beans or asparagus instead or in addition to the peppers)
1 red onion peeled, halved and cut into very thin slices
100g feta cheese crumbled
1 large handful of fresh basil or mint
4 sticks of celery sliced with the leaves left nearly whole
**For the dressing**
4 tablespoons olive oil
1 teaspoon tomato puree
1 teaspoon paprika
2 tablespoons red wine vinegar
Salt and pepper

**Method**
1. preheat the oven to 200 with a baking tin inside
2. cut the bread into rough squares about the size of a golf ball
3. place the bread in a bowl, sprinkle over the olive oil then toss it around to get a good coating
4. put the tomatoes on top of the bread and bake in the oven in the baking tin turning once when the bread is crisp and golden on top
5. while the bread is cooling make the dressing by shaking all the ingredients vigorously in a screw-top jar
6. mix the bread, tomatoes, pepper, celery, onion and feta in a bowl, spoon over the dressing, toss lightly and serve

# COUSCOUS

Serves 4 as a main course
Takes 60 minutes

**Ingredients**
275g couscous
125g halloumi cheese crumbled
1 yellow or orange pepper cut into pieces about 2cm square
1 red pepper cut into pieces about 2cm square
1 small aubergine cut into 1cm squares
1 large courgette or 2 smaller ones cut into 1cm squares
2 medium-sized red onions peeled and cut into quarters
250g cherry tomatoes
100g pine nuts
50g sultanas
1 handful fresh basil leaves
2 tablespoons green pesto sauce
3 tablespoons olive oil (preferably not extra virgin)
1 handful fresh coriander leaves coarsely chopped
Salt and pepper

**For the dressing**
4 tablespoons olive oil
2 teaspoons tomato puree
1 level teaspoon paprika
1 level teaspoon ground cumin
1 level teaspoon cinnamon
2 tablespoons lemon juice

**Method**
1. pre-heat the oven to 240C
2. shake the dressing ingredients vigorously in a screw-top jar
3. put the peppers, aubergine, courgette, onion, torn basil leaves and tomatoes in a bowl, sprinkle with salt and pepper, drizzle over the olive oil and then mix with your hands to give all the vegetables a good coating. Put in a baking tin in the oven for 15 minutes then give them a gentle stir, check they aren't burning

and sprinkle over the halloumi cheese, sultanas and pine nuts before returning to the oven for another 10 minutes or until they look done and the cheese and pine nuts have browned a bit. Stir in the pesto sauce and allow to cool.

4. meanwhile cook the couscous according to the instructions on the packet, add the coriander and fluff it up with a fork, then gently stir in the cooked items and serve the dressing separately.

# SALADE NICOISE

There are loads of different versions of this classic Provencal salad and it practically qualifies as an enthusiastic salad on its own, although it seems that it should contain potatoes, green beans, tuna, eggs and anchovies. You can make it with tinned tuna or fresh tuna but I prefer the yellow fin tuna which comes in oil in a jar.

Preparation time 45 minutes
Serves 4-6

200g jar of yellow fin tuna in oil
500g small salad potatoes
6 spring onions finely chopped or half a red onion finely chopped
400g green beans
2 lettuces such as Lollo Rosso and Cos washed and dried
4 ripe tomatoes
4 hard boiled eggs shelled and halved
1 small jar or 50g tin of anchovies in oil
20 black olives
2 tablespoons capers rinsed under the tap
Fresh basil
Fresh tarragon and chervil chopped finely
1 teaspoon dried thyme

**For the dressing for the potatoes**
4 tablespoons extra virgin olive oil *
2 tablespoons lemon juice
1 teaspoon Dijon mustard
Salt and pepper

**For the dressing for the beans and lettuce**
4 tablespoons extra virgin olive oil
2 tablespoons red wine vinegar
1 teaspoon honey or sugar
Salt and pepper

**Method**

1. make the two types of dressing shaking in a jar or stirring in a bowl with a fork
2. cook the potatoes in salted boiling water until tender (about 15 minutes), drain and while still warm mix in a bowl with the chopped onions and the dressing. Break up the potatoes a little with a fork as you do this. Sprinkle the potatoes with dried thyme
3. cook the beans in boiling water until firm but tender (about 5 minutes), drain and refresh under the cold tap then toss with a couple of tablespoons of the second dressing
4. arrange the lettuce leaves on a large platter, or if you don't have one large enough make up separate plates for each diner. Make separate little piles of each ingredient – beans on top of the potatoes, sliced tomatoes with some torn basil and olive oil (here's where extra virgin would be better) drizzled over, the eggs with two anchovy fillets on each half, a heap of tuna, 5 olives each so everyone is a rich man, not a beggar-man or thief and a small heap of capers, which go very well with the tuna, so put them next to it..
5. scatter over the tarragon and chervil if you have it, especially on the eggs

*(there is a lot of fuss about extra virgin olive oil – some people regard it as a "must have" for everything.  In fact apart from being considerably more expensive it is best used for salads and dressings rather than cooking (it is said to burn in cooking although I've never been quite sure about that))

# MOULES A LA CREME

Serves 4
Takes 30 minutes

**Ingredients**
2 kg mussels
2 shallots finely chopped
2 garlic cloves finely chopped
20g butter
A handful of flat leaf parsley finely chopped
Small bunch of fresh thyme
2 bay leaves
100ml dry white wine
100ml double cream
French bread

**Method**
1. wash the mussels in cold water and discard any that have cracked shells or which don't close when tapped sharply on the work-surface
2. pull out the fibrous beards and cut off any barnacles with a knife. Rinse again and check that you got all the beards off.
3. melt the butter in a large pan with a tight-fitting lid and soften the garlic and shallots in it
4. pour in the mussels, the bay leaves, thyme and the wine, turn up the heat to high and put the cover on the pan
5. give the pan a shake every minute or so and open the lid after 3 minutes to see if the mussels have opened wide. If they haven't opened give the pan another shake and give them another minute.
6. when they have opened, (discard any odd ones that haven't) remove the pan from the heat, remove the bay leaves and thyme and pour in the cream and sprinkle the parsley

7. ladle into bowls and serve with plenty of crusty French bread bread.

# BAKED AUBERGINE AND TOMATO

Serves 4

Easy to make but allow 60 minutes or longer if you want to eat it cold

## Ingredients

2 medium aubergines
4 tablespoons olive oil
1 large onion
2 cloves garlic
1 teaspoon ground cumin
1 teaspoon ground cinnamon
1 large handful of pine nuts
3 tablespoons tomato puree
6 large tomatoes
2 teaspoons dried oregano
3 tablespoons grated parmesan or cheddar
5 tablespoons fresh breadcrumbs
Salt and pepper

## Method

1. slice the vegetables thinly.  If you want to, sprinkle salt over the aubergine slices and leave for 30 minutes then rinse off the salt and dry the slices. I don't think it is worth it.
2. heat the oven to 200C and heat the grill
3. heat 2 tablespoons of olive oil in a fairly hot frying pan and fry the onion with the cumin and cinnamon until soft and golden. When that is nearly soft add the garlic, tomato puree and pine nuts.
4. while the onions are cooking place the aubergine slices on the grill pan, brush with olive oil and grill until browned then turn over and repeat.
5. in an oven-proof dish place a layer of tomatoes and sprinkle with oregano and pepper, then a layer of aubergine slices

with a sprinkling of oregano and pepper and then a layer of onion mixture. Repeat the process until all the vegetables are used up but finish with a layer of tomatoes on top and drizzle them with the rest of the oil.

6. bake in the oven for 20 minutes, mix the cheese and breadcrumbs together, then sprinkle the cheese and breadcrumbs over the top and bake for another 10 minutes.

# CANNELLINI BEANS WITH CHORIZO

Serves 4
Takes 25 minutes

## Ingredients
400g cannelloni beans from a jar or can
200g chorizo sausage (the cooking type which is softer and sold whole not the dried salami type, although if that is all you can get you can use it)
3 tablespoons olive oil
2 garlic cloves finely chopped
1 level teaspoon paprika (if you can get Pimenton, the smoked Spanish variety so much the better)
2 tablespoons coarsely chopped coriander
1 level teaspoon salt

## Method
1. rinse the beans in a colander
2. cut the chorizo into slices
3. heat the olive oil in a large pan and fry the chorizo until browned and the colour is released into the oil. Remove the chorizo then add the paprika and stir for a minute or two before adding the beans, garlic and salt.
4. heat the beans gently and when warm stir in the coriander and chorizo.
5. serve

# COURGETTE SALAD

This has something of a Moorish flavour.
Serves 4 as a side dish or starter
20 minutes to make but needs to "marinate" for at least 3 hours

## Ingredients
500g courgettes sliced about 1 centimetre thick
1 garlic clove peeled and crushed slightly
3 tablespoons Olive oil
50g pine kernels
50g raisins or sultanas
3 tablespoons chopped mint
1 tablespoon lemon juice
Salt and pepper

## Method
1. heat the oil in a frying pan and fry the garlic until golden then remove it and discard.
2. fry the courgette slices gently until tender but firm, turning once
3. stir all the ingredients together in a large bowl and taste for seasoning adjusting according to your taste
4. leave in a cool place to absorb the flavours until ready to eat

# RICE WITH PRAWNS AND CHORIZO

Serves 4
Takes 30 minutes

## Ingredients
3 tablespoons olive oil
1 large onion chopped
2 red peppers cored, de-seeded and chopped
2 garlic cloves peeled and chopped
2 large tomatoes peeled, de-seeded and chopped
200g long grain rice
200g chorizo cooking sausage cut into slices
450 ml chicken stock
450g uncooked large prawns

## Method
1. peel the prawns and then with a sharp knife cut down the backs and remove any black intestine. Rinse thoroughly and dry.
2. heat the oil in a large saucepan and fry the chorizo, onion and peppers adding the garlic when the other vegetables are nearly soft and frying for a minute or two more
3. add the tomatoes and fry for 1 minute
4. add the rice and cook, stirring for 2 minutes then add the stock and bring to the boil
5. turn down the heat, cover the pan and simmer for about 15 minutes until the rice is tender but still with some liquid
6. add the prawns, stir, replace the lid and after about 5 minutes the prawns should be pink and the surplus liquid absorbed by the rice. If the rice is still too wet give it a stir and cook a while longer with the lid off.

# GREEK SALAD

Serves 4
Takes about 20 minutes

## Ingredients
1 Cos lettuce washed and dried
4 large ripe tomatoes skinned, de-seeded and quartered
1 cucumber peeled and thickly sliced
1 mild onion very thinly sliced and then the slices pushed into rings
2 red or yellow peppers cored, de-seeded and cut into thin slices, or rings if you're clever
200g Feta cheese cut into long narrow oblongs
20 black olives
2 tablespoons chopped mint
1 level teaspoon of dried marjoram or oregano
## Dressing
6 tablespoons olive oil
2 tablespoons lemon juice
Salt and pepper

## Method
1. Tear the lettuce leaves and arrange on 4 plates to form a base for the other ingredients
2. arrange the other vegetables and then place the cheese on top
3. shake the dressing ingredients in a jar with a screw top until blended
4. drizzle the dressing over the salad, including the cheese, then sprinkle the marjoram or oregano over the cheese

# PIZZA

Of course you can go down to the nearest pizzeria and personally that is what I would recommend, especially if they do "pizza au feu du bois" like my daughter's favourite restaurant in all the world, Le Figuier in Corsica which does wonderful pizzas under the spreading leaves of a huge fig tree, but this is quite fun to make and kneading dough is very therapeutic.

Serves 4

## Ingredients

### Base
350g strong plain flour
½ teaspoon salt
1 sachet easy-blend dried yeast
A pinch of caster sugar
2 tablespoons olive oil

### Topping
400g can of tomatoes pieces
100g thin slices of salami
1 mild onion thinly sliced
12 black olives
2   ripe tomatoes thinly sliced
100g mozzarella very thinly sliced
2 teaspoons oregano

## Method
1. heat the oven to 220C/gas mark 7
2. simmer the canned tomatoes in a saucepan uncovered, stirring occasionally until reduced to a paste-like consistency
3. stir the flour, salt, yeast and sugar in a large bowl. Mix the oil with 200ml of tepid water. Make a well in the centre of the flour

mix and pour the oil and water in bit by bit, pushing the flour mix into the liquid and gradually forming it all into a dough.

4. knead the dough on a lightly floured surface until elastic (about 10 minutes). Roll out to a 30cm circle (use a bottle if you don't have a rolling-pin) and place on an oiled baking sheet

5. spread the cooked tomatoes over the base and then arrange the other ingredients on top, sprinkling with oregano. Cook in the oven for 20 minutes.

# FRIED PEAS WITH BACON

Serves 4  if you fill the chinks with cheese, salami etc..
Takes 20 minutes

## Ingredients
500g frozen peas
150 g bacon cut into lardons
1 onion sliced
1 glass of white wine
Fresh bread crumbs
50g butter
1 tablespoon olive oil

## Method
1. fry the onion and the pancetta in half the butter and the olive oil until the onion is soft and the pancetta is crisp
2  add the wine and let it bubble then add the peas
3. after 5 minutes the wine should have evaporated so add rest of the butter and when that is melted and foaming, the breadcrumbs
4. Serve when the breadcrumbs are golden.

# SPANISH OMELETTE (TORTILLA)

Serves 4

Takes 25 minutes

## Ingredients

150 ml olive oil

2 very large potatoes sliced about ½ centimeter thick

2 large onions peeled, cut in half and finely sliced

6 large eggs

Salt and pepper

## Method

1. Heat the oil in a frying pan and fry the onions gently
2. meanwhile cook the potato slices in salted water until parboiled ( cooked but still firm – test with the point of a knife)
3. drain the potatoes and add them to the onions in the frying pan. Stir gently together so the potatoes absorb some onion flavour.
4. beat the eggs in a large bowl with plenty of black pepper
5. when the onions and potatoes are cooked take off the heat and allow to cool slightly then tip them into the eggs and mix together
6. quickly give the frying pan a wipe out with kitchen towel, add a little more olive oil (enough to make the surface non-stick but not too much) and then put the frying pan on a low heat until you can see a slight haze
7. tip the egg mixture into the pan and spread out and flatten the contents with a spatula. Shake pan gently from time to time to ensure the omelette is not sticking and use a palette knife to check that the bottom is not browning too much.
8. pre-heat the grill
9. after about 8 minutes when the omelette has solidified a bit it is time to cook the other side. The easy way to do this is to place the frying pan under a hot grill for about 5 minutes. If you are of a Spanish toreador mentality you may prefer to hold a plate over the frying pan, invert the pan with the plate firmly in place, so

the omelette lands on the plate and then slide the omelette back into the frying pan the other way up and continue cooking.
10. either way turn the omelette out onto a plate when cooked and eat either hot or cold.

# FRITTATA

A frittata is the showy Italian cousin of the tortilla.
Serves 4
Takes 25 minutes

**Ingredients**
4 tablespoons olive oil
4 large tomatoes sliced*
6 large eggs
Salt and pepper

**Method**
1. Heat the oil in a frying pan and fry the tomatoes gently for about 10 minutes until tender
2. beat the eggs in a large bowl with plenty of black pepper
3. add the cooked tomatoes to the eggs and mix together
4. give the frying pan a wipe out with kitchen towel, add 2 tablespoons olive oil and then put the frying pan on a medium heat until the oil sizzles
5. tip the egg mixture into the pan and spread out and flatten the contents with a spatula. Cook for about 8 minutes shaking pan gently from time to time to ensure the frittata is not sticking or the underside browning too much.
6. pre-heat the grill if using (see below)
7. after about 8 minutes when the omelette has solidified a bit it is time to cook the other side. The easy way to do this is to place the frying pan under a hot grill for about 5 minutes. If you prefer the riskier alternative (or don't have a grill) hold a plate over the frying pan, invert the pan with the plate firmly in place, so the omelette lands on the plate and then slide the omelette back into the frying pan the other way up and continue cooking.
8. either way turn the omelette out onto a plate when cooked and eat either hot or cold.

\*   if you prefer you can substitute onions, peas, courgettes, peppers or a combination

# PINARELLO OMELETTE

A really tasty take on a traditional omelette.
Takes 10 minutes

**Ingredients**
For each omelette:
3 eggs
50g butter
1 tablespoon olive oil
Half a ripe avocado sliced
1 heaped tablespoon of bacon lardons (if ready made lardons are not available cut streaky bacon into small pieces)
1 dessertspoon of fresh chives snipped into small pieces
1 dessertspoon of chopped sun-dried tomatoes
Black pepper

**Method**
1. Heat the oil in a frying pan and fry the bacon lardons on a high heat until crispy, then dry them on kitchen paper
2. use a fork to beat the eggs well in a large bowl with a few turns of black pepper
3. Add the sun-dried tomatoes and chives to the eggs and mix together
4 give the frying pan a wipe out with kitchen towel, and then put the frying pan on a medium heat
5. when the pan is warm (hold your hand a couple of inches above it to see) drop the butter into the pan. ( It should sizzle immediately, if it doesn't your pan isn't warm enough and if it browns and burns instantly it is too hot. In either case wipe out the pan with a wad of kitchen towel and adjust the heat. The right temperature is vital for a good omelette.)
6. Give the butter a quick stir so it foams and then without waiting for it all to melt, tip in the egg mixture and with a spatula push it from the edges toward the middle of the pan so that you create a low

hill in the middle. Rock the pan a little so that the egg mixture spreads to the sides and starts to set.

7 sprinkle the lardons over the open omelette and place the avocado slices in a row just one side of the centre.

8. as soon as the omelette is nearly set slide it onto a plate and fold it over the avocado. Serve immediately with crusty bread to mop up the plate.

# TSATSIKI

Serves 4 as a side dish
Takes 15 minutes

## Ingredients
2 continental size cucumbers or 1 British peeled and diced
1 teaspoon salt
300ml plain creamy Greek style yoghurt
1 clove garlic peeled and very finely chopped (use a garlic press if you have one)
1 tablespoon olive oil
1 teaspoon white wine vinegar
Pepper
2 tablespoons finely chopped mint

## Method
1. put the cucumber pieces in a bowl and sprinkle in the salt. Leave for 15 minutes.
2. in another bowl mix together the yoghurt, garlic, oil and vinegar
3. drain as much water as possible from the cucumber and press it gently between a dry cloth or kitchen towel then fold into the yoghurt mixture.
4. season to taste with salt and pepper and stir in the mint before serving

# HOT GOATS CHEESE SALAD

Serves 4
Takes 15 minutes

**Ingredients**
A piece of cylindrical shaped goats cheese about 4 inches (10 centimetres) long
1 loaf of French bread of the same or slightly greater width as the goats cheese
100g pine nuts
1 nice lettuce washed and shaken to dry
Balsamic vinegar dressing or vinaigrette (see dressings)
Pepper

**Method**
1. heat the oven to 180 degrees
2. slice the french bread crossways into rounds, allowing three pieces per person
3. place the bread on an oven tray and place a slice of goats cheese about a third of an inch (half a centimeter) thick on each piece of bread
4. put the bread into the oven for 10 minutes, but check after 5
5. toast the pine nuts to a golden brown in a dry frying pan on a medium-high heat. Stir them around and don't take your eye off them because they burn in an instant.
6. place the lettuce leaves on 4 plates, place 3 pieces of the hot bread and goats cheese on top as soon as it is ready, scatter over the pine nuts and drizzle with the dressing. Serve immediately.

# CHORIZO IN RED WINE

Serves 4
Takes 15 minutes

**Ingredients**
400g of chorizo (the soft cooking variety, not the much thicker
salami-like variety) cut into slices ¼ of an inch thick
A small glass of red wine
1 tbsp chopped parsley
1 tbsp olive oil
**Method**

1. heat the olive oil in a frying pan and fry the chorizo slices for about 5 minutes until brown and a bit crispy, then turn and do the other side
2. take the pan off the heat and add the wine
3. return to the heat and deglaze (i.e. scrape the bottom of the pan to loosen any crusty bits)
4. let the wine thicken a bit (only takes a minute or two) and scatter the parsley over it
5. pour into a dish and serve with bread to mop up the sauce

# SUPPER RECIPES

## STARTERS

Bearing in mind that you are on holiday, didn't have room to pack the candelabras and that the aim of this book is to feed the family relaxed and informal meals, rather than spend the entire vacation preparing a six course dinner (after all that's what restaurants are for), you may want to skip starters. However here are a few really easy ones. In fact most are so easy they don't need a recipe.

| EASY |
|---|
| Melon, with or without parma ham |
| Parma ham with figs |
| Freshly cooked prawns with mayonnaise (see recipe in the dressings chapter) |
| Pate (bought) with cornichons (small gherkins) |
| A green salad with a vinaigrette dressing (see recipe in the dressings chapter) |
| An hors d'oeuvre of olives, grilled artichokes, grilled peppers, salami |
| Avocado with vinaigrette dressing |
| Smoked salmon |
| Asparagus<br>Plunge the asparagus into salted boiling water for 8-10 minutes until tender but not soft, plunge into cold water, drain and serve with mayonnaise or vinaigrette dressing. |
| **REQUIRE SLIGHTLY MORE EFFORT** |
| Salade frisee aux lardons<br>Wash and dry 1 frisee lettuce and put in a bowl, gently fry a large handful of bacon lardons until the fat runs and they turn crispy, tip this over the lettuce then quickly add two tablespoons of red wine vinegar to the remaining fat in the hot pan, let it bubble and pour this over the lettuce as well, give the lettuce a good stir and serve. |
| Crudités<br>Batons of peeled raw cucumber, small/medium carrots, celery, red or yellow pepper de-seeded, pith removed and cut into thin sticks, served |

with mayonnaise (see recipe in the dressings chapter) or an anchovy dip made by pounding the contents of a tin of anchovies with a crushed clove of garlic, some pepper and more olive oil.

## Prawns in garlic

Heat 150ml olive oil in a frying pan, toss in 4 cloves of finely chopped garlic and a large pinch of paprika, turn around in the oil and as it begins to colour put the unpeeled prawns in the sizzling oil and stir for 2 minutes turning so they go pink on both sides. Serve with French bread and plenty of paper towels.

## Insalata tricolore

Slices of ripe avocado, tomatoes and buffalo mozzarella cheese drizzled with a thick dressing made by shaking in a screw top jar 12 tablespoons of extra virgin olive oil with 3 tablespoons of lemon juice and one tablespoon of runny honey or sugar with salt and pepper to taste.

# SUPPER RECIPES

## MAIN COURSES

| RECIPE | PAGE |
|---|---|
| Spaghetti alla Pomodori | 44 |
| Spaghetti alla Putanesca | 45 |
| Penny's penne with mozzarella and tomato | 46 |
| Paella | 47 |
| Lamb Tagine | 49 |
| Lamb Pilaff | 51 |
| Pork with sage and capers | 53 |
| Lamb with rosemary, anchovies and garlic | 55 |
| Steak | 57 |
| Chicken with garlic | 59 |
| Chicken a la Nicoise | 61 |
| Grilled sardines | 63 |
| Roasted Sea Bass | 65 |
| Moroccan Fish fillets | 66 |
| Chicken Fajitas | 68 |
| Lamb Curry | 69 |
| Pork Spare Ribs | 70 |
| Cheating : Poulet Roti | 71 |

# SPAGHETTI ALLA POMODORI

This has a lot more flavour than you would expect.
Serves 4 as a main course.
Time: 30 minutes

**Ingredients**
2x 350g cans of tomatoes
100 ml olive oil
4 cloves of garlic
4 handfuls of fresh basil leaves
1 level teaspoon of dried oregano
Red wine
Salt
Pepper
500g dried spaghetti
100g parmesan cheese

**Method**
1. Heat the oil in a saucepan on medium heat.
2. peel and slice the garlic cloves and place in the oil when hot and cook until they start to take colour, then off the heat add the tomatoes
3. return the saucepan to the heat and add the oregano and tear up the basil leaves and drop them in too. Add a splash or two of red wine.
4. allow the sauce to bubble gently for 20 minutes, stirring occasionally,
5. taste the tomato sauce for seasoning and add salt and pepper to taste
6. bring a large pan of water to the boil and add a few drops of olive oil (it stops the spaghetti sticking together especially if your pan isn't that large)
7. cook the spaghetti according to the instructions on the packet and drain it
8. add 50g of parmesan to the tomato sauce, stir well then add the spaghetti and stir together for a minute or two
9. serve and pass around the rest of the parmesan.

# SPAGHETTI ALLA PUTANESCA

Takes 30 minutes
Serves 4
**Ingredients**
5 tablespoons olive oil
50g butter
2 cloves of garlic finely chopped
50g tin of anchovies
2 tablespoons capers
150g black olives
350g tin of tomatoes
2 tablespoons finely chopped parsley or basil
1 small chilli pepper de-seeded and finely chopped
400g spaghetti
Salt and pepper

**Method**
1. heat the oil and butter in a large saucepan and tip in the tin of anchovies with the oil they are in
2. sauté, breaking up the anchovies then add the garlic
3. when the garlic is taking colour add the tomatoes, chilli, capers and olives
4. simmer for 20 minutes, taste for seasoning and add pepper (and salt if needed, although the anchovies may contain enough salt)
5. cook the spaghetti until nearly cooked, drain and add to the sauce in the saucepan and cook together for 5 minutes
6. stir in the parsley or basil
7. serve

# PENNY's PENNE PASTA WITH MOZZARELLA AND TOMATO

Takes 30 minutes
Serves 4
**Ingredients**
400g penne pasta
5 tablespoons olive oil
1 garlic clove peeled and squashed
350g tin of chopped tomatoes
1 level teaspoon of dried oregano
200g mozzarella cheese thinly sliced
100g grated parmesan
A large handful of fresh basil leaves
Salt and pepper

**Method**
1. pre-heat the oven to 230 $^0$C
2. bring a large saucepan of salted water to the boil, add the pasta and cook for 1-2 minutes less than the time on the packet because the pasta will be cooked some more in the oven
3. meanwhile heat the oil in a separate large saucepan on a high heat and when hot add the garlic and stir it round for a minute or so until golden then remove it and discard
4. off the heat add the tomatoes, half the mozzarella, half the parmesan and the oregano. Season with salt and pepper.
5. return to the heat and cook stirring frequently for 10 minutes.
6. drain the pasta and tip it into the sauce
7. add the basil and give it all a good stir then tip it into an oven-proof dish, top with the remainder of the mozzarella and parmesan and place in the oven for 15 minutes.
8. remove and serve

# PAELLA

Serves 4

Allow an hour and a half to make this – but it is a real feast

Needs to be made in a wok or very large frying pan and if it doesn't have a lid you will need to cover with a double layer of kitchen foil at stage 8 below.

## Ingredients

1 level dessertspoon of saffron threads
300g short grain paella rice
16 clams or mussels
4 chicken thighs
100g chorizo sliced into small slices
1 large onion
1 red pepper cored and cut into 1 cm squares
3 garlic cloves finely chopped
1 teaspoon pimenton or mild paprika
100g frozen peas
900ml chicken stock
16 uncooked prawns peeled, cut along the back and the black intestine removed and washed

## Method

1. put the saffron into a cup and fill with hot water, leave to infuse
2. discard any clams or mussels which do not close when tapped sharply. Remove the beards of any mussels and scrape off any barnacles then rinse
3. fry the chicken thighs and the chorizo in the paella pan in 3 tablespoons oil until the chicken is golden, set aside
4. add another 3 tablespoons of the oil and fry the onions and peppers for 3 minutes then add the garlic and paprika and fry for a further 3 minutes or so until the onions are soft
5. add the rice and peas to the pan and stir so every grain of rice is coated

6. add the saffron liquid and stir again, then the stock and bring to the boil stirring
7. turn down the heat and simmer uncovered until most of the liquid is absorbed but the rice is still moist
8. place the clams or mussels on top of the rice, cover and continue cooking until the shell-fish have opened and the prawns are pink
9. discard any shell-fish which have not opened
10. serve

# LAMB TAGINE

Serves 8

Allow two and a half hours to make this – but only 30 minutes of that is preparation, the rest is slow cooking. This really suits being made the day before and re-heating so is great for dinner parties, which is why I have stepped up the amounts to serve 8.

You will need a cast iron casserole or a wok with a well-fitting lid which can go from the top of the stove into the oven.

## Ingredients

1 level teaspoon of saffron threads
2 tablespoons olive oil
1 kilo lamb neck fillets cut into 2 cm pieces across the fillet
2 large onions chopped
3 garlic cloves finely chopped
1 glass white wine
1 tablespoon mild paprika
1 teaspoon ground ginger
1 teaspoon ground cinnamon
½ teaspoon hot chilli powder
200g dried ready to eat apricots or you can substitute sultanas
2 tablespoons runny honey
1 can chopped tomatoes

## Method

1. put the saffron into a cup and fill with hot water, leave to infuse
2. pre-heat the oven to 160 $^0$C
3. heat the oil in the casserole and brown the lamb pieces well on a medium-high heat. Do this in batches and don't let the pieces touch each other or it will take ages. Remove the lamb pieces as you go. If the pan gets too dry add a bit more oil.
4. when the lamb is all browned lower the heat, pour in the wine and scrape the pan to remove any crusty bits, then add the onions and garlic, cover the pan and cook gently for 10 minutes until the onions are soft.

5. empty the cup in which the saffron has been infusing into the pan and chuck in the rest of the ingredients, tomatoes last. Give them all a good stir.
6. turn up the heat and bring to the boil then cover with the lid and put in the preheated oven for 2 hours.
7. remove and taste for seasoning adding salt and pepper to taste.
8. I like this with plain boiled potatoes, a bowl of plain Greek yoghurt and boiled green beans but for a more exotic touch serve it with plain couscous cooked in accordance with the packet instructions (perhaps with some browned pine nuts and chopped coriander added) and tsatsiki (see the recipe in this book).

# LAMB PILAFF

Serves 4
Takes  1.5 hours

## Ingredients
3 tablespoons olive oil
1 large onion peeled and chopped
500g lean boneless lamb cut into pieces the size of a large grape
50g pine nuts
1 teaspoon cumin
50g sultanas
Salt and pepper
2 teaspoons cinnamon
3 tablespoons finely chopped flat leaf parsley
3 tablespoons tomato puree
500g long grain easy cook rice

## Method
1. heat the oil in a large saucepan or frying pan and fry the onions until softened
2. add the lamb and the cumin and cinnamon, fry turning until the lamb is browned all over
3. brown the pine nuts in a separate pan without oil (stir them about and watch they don't burn) and add them to the lamb
4. stir in the sultanas, tomato puree and parsley
5. just cover with water, stir, bring to the boil and simmer until the lamb is really tender (about 45 minutes). If it dries out add more water.
6. add the rice and stir well then cover with water and stir again
7. simmer very gently, covered, without stirring for 15 minutes or until the rice is cooked and the water has been absorbed
8. add salt and pepper and stir again
9. serve

# PORK WITH SAGE AND CAPERS

This has a light and delicate flavour.

Serves 4
Takes 2 hours

**Ingredients**
1 kg boned loin of pork cut into cubes 2cm square
3 tablespoons olive oil
2 onions peeled and chopped
150 ml white wine
1 tablespoon fresh sage chopped
2 sprigs fresh thyme
2 bay leaves
100 ml dry vermouth
2 tablespoons capers
1 tablespoon flat leaf parsley finely chopped

**Method**
1. heat the oil in a large saucepan
2. rub the meat with salt and pepper and brown it on all sides*
3. remove the meat from the pan and set aside
4. fry the onions in the pan until softened (about 5 minutes)
5. add the wine and scrape the bottom of the pan to loosen any burnt-on bits
6. return the meat to the pan with the sage, thyme and bay leaves
7. stir, cover the pan with a tight fitting lid (use cooking foil to seal the pan if necessary) and cook gently for 1 hour 15 minutes until the pork is tender. If it dries out during cooking add a little water.
8. when the meat is cooked lift it out with a slotted spoon, add the vermouth and bring to the boil stirring well and loosening any sediment
9. return the meat to the pan with the capers, remove the bay leaves and thyme sprigs and heat through
10. check the seasoning and serve sprinkled with parsley, with plain boiled potatoes and green salad

* Note: when browning meat, the pieces should not be packed tightly together otherwise it takes forever. If necessary brown it in batches small enough to keep the pieces separate.

# LAMB WITH ROSEMARY GARLIC AND ANCHOVY

A hearty and full-flavoured Provencal dish but not as garlicky as you might think.

Serves 4-6 depending on the size of the leg of lamb.
Takes only 20 minutes preparation but then allow 3 hours for marinating and 1-1½ hours for cooking.

**Ingredients**
2 tablespoons olive oil
1 teaspoon dried rosemary
1 teaspoon dried thyme
1 teaspoon salt
1 teaspoon black pepper
1 leg of lamb
12 garlic cloves peeled
12 anchovy fillets cut in half crossways
150 ml white wine
1 tablespoon finely chopped flat leaf parsley

**Method**
1. cut 6 of the garlic cloves into slivers
2. stab a pointed knife into the leg of lamb and push into the hole an anchovy half and a sliver of garlic. Repeat the process all over the leg of lamb until the anchovies and slivers have been used up
3. mix the olive oil, thyme, rosemary and salt and pepper and rub this all over the leg of lamb
4. leave the lamb to marinate for 3 hours
5. heat the oven to $220^0$C/gas mark 7
6. place the lamb in a roasting tin in the centre of the oven and roast for 20 minutes then reduce the oven temperature to $190^0$C/gas mark 5 for 20 minutes per 500g . Check whether

it is done enough for your taste by cutting into the leg after 40 minutes at the lower temperature.

7.  while the meat is cooking stew the remaining cloves of garlic gently in a little water in a small saucepan until soft. (about 15 minutes). When cooked drain off the water and mash the garlic to a paste with a fork or the back of a spoon.

8.  when the meat is cooked remove it from the pan and allow to rest for 10 minutes.

9.  put the roasting tin on a low heat on top of the cooker, add the wine and allow it to bubble, scraping well to deglaze the pan, then stir in the mashed garlic and when that has been mixed in, the parsley .

10. carve the lamb and pour the gravy over it before serving.

# STEAK

Everyone has their views and theories on steak! Rare or well done? Fillet or rump? Grilled or fried? Seasoned with salt before cooking or not? Marinade or not? Better with a sauce? Everyone is right but here is one simple way of cooking steak.

Serves 4
Takes 15 minutes, plus marinading, and the time for the preparation of the accompaniments.

## Ingredients
4 rump steaks about 225 grams and 2-3 cm thick
Olive oil
Red wine vinegar
2 cloves garlic finely chopped
4 heaped teaspoons of Herbes de Provence (these mixtures of dried aromatic herbs are sold in small jars in many supermarkets in the UK and abroad. The contents can vary and so can the proportions but savory, wild thyme, rosemary, marjoram, basil and oregano are typical)
Salt and pepper
4 rounded dessertspoons of butter soft enough to spread easily
4 rounded teaspoons of Dijon mustard

## Method
1. put the steaks in a flat dish, mix together 2 tablespoons of olive oil and 2 tablespoons of red wine vinegar and drizzle the steaks then half the garlic. Turn the steaks over to ensure a good coating. Leave to marinate in the fridge for 1-3 hours.
2. mix the butter, mustard and Herbes de Provence together in a bowl
3. pre-heat the grill or barbeque (if a barbeque the coals or wood should have a layer of white ash on top of the red coals).
4. if you don't have a grill or barbeque heat a frying pan with a little oil in it until just smoking

5. season the steaks well with salt and pepper, spread a good scraping of the herb butter on the side which will be cooked first and put it on the heat for two minutes, spread another scraping of butter on the uncooked side of the steak before turning it over. Cook for another two minutes. These should be done enough to suit those who like their steaks rare but it depends on factors like the size and thickness of the steak, the heat of the grill or frying pan and the distance from the heat if grilling. The best test is to press it with your finger or the flat side of a fork. A rare steak is soft, a medium is firm but yielding and a well-done steak is firm. If you aren't sure, cut into the steak to check and cook it for longer if desired.
6. let the steaks rest for 3 minutes in a warm place before serving.
7. at home in the UK I like to serve with mashed potatoes into which I have stirred one finely chopped spring onion per person and peas. In a warmer climate potato salad and a green salad go well.

# CHICKEN WITH GARLIC

This is a wonderfully fragrant and easy dish. The garlic turns into a paste inside its skin and can be removed by pressing on the clove with a knife before spreading on the toast. It loses all its sharpness in the cooking.

Serves 4
Takes 15 minutes to prepare and 60-90 minutes to cook

**Ingredients**
1 roasting chicken trussed, about 1.75kg
2 large sprigs fresh rosemary
2 large sprigs fresh thyme
2 bay leaves
2 tablespoons olive oil
150 ml white wine
20 cloves of garlic unpeeled
Salt and pepper
12 slices of French bread
Kitchen foil

**Method**
1. preheat the oven to 190C/gas mark 5
2. Heat the oil on top of the stove in a flameproof casserole with a lid which can go in the oven
3. rub the chicken inside and out with plenty of salt and pepper and stuff one bay leaf, rosemary sprig and thyme sprig in the cavity
4. brown the chicken all over in the hot oil.
5. take the casserole off the heat and remove the chicken
6. pour in the wine and scrape around to loosen any stuck on bits
7. throw in the garlic cloves and put the chicken on top of them and put the remaining herbs on top of the chicken
8. put kitchen foil over the top of the casserole before placing on the lid to ensure it is sealed and put it in the oven

9. cook for 60 minutes then check by sticking a knife into the inside fleshy part of the leg and the breast and seeing if the juices run clear. If not cook for longer.
10. toast the bread
11. carve the chicken giving everyone 5 cloves of garlic which they can spread on the toast and  pouring the sauce from the casserole on the chicken slices.
12. serve with green salad.

# CHICKEN A LA NICOISE

Serves 4

Takes 1 hour

This is a real crowd pleaser. One pot cookery saves the washing up and it keeps warm well while you serve a first course.

## Ingredients

4 chicken joints – large boned thighs are easiest
1 clove garlic peeled and sliced
Salt and pepper
2 tablespoons olive oil
2 onions peeled and thinly sliced
2 red peppers and 1 yellow cut into strips
1 small glass of red wine
400g tomatoes skinned, de-seeded and chopped or a can of chopped tomatoes
20 black olives
1 tablespoon of chopped parsley to serve

## Method

1. rub the chicken pieces with salt and pepper
2. heat the oil in a large saucepan or wok and brown the chicken pieces all over, do two at a time if the pan is too crowded
3. remove the chicken, lower the heat and fry the onions until golden and soft
4. add the peppers and garlic and cook for 5 minutes
5. tip in the tomatoes, raise the heat and cook for 5 minutes until the sauce is slightly thickened.
6. Deglaze the pan with a small glass of red wine. (i.e. pour in the wine and scrape any crusty bits off the bottom of the pan.
7. return the chicken pieces, cover the pan and cook over a moderate heat for 30 minutes
8. add the olives and heat for a further 5 minutes
9. check that the chicken is done by sticking the point of a knife in the thickest part and if the juices run yellow with no trace of pink it is done

10. serve with plain boiled potatoes, sprinkled with parsley. (if the potatoes are cooked before you are ready to serve just put them in with the chicken to keep warm.

# GRILLED SARDINES

Serves 4

Takes 10 minute plus the time to prepare the sardines if the fishmonger has not done that for you.

## Ingredients

12 fresh sardines, or 16 if they are small (fresh sardines should have bright eyes and shiny scales)
3 tablespoons olive oil
1 garlic clove chopped very small
1 small red chilli de-seeded and chopped very small
Salt and pepper

## Method

1. put the garlic and chilli into the olive oil to infuse
2. pre-heat the grill to high. If barbequing ensure there is a layer of grey ash over the red coals
3. brush the sardines with plenty of oil and sprinkle with salt and pepper
4. grill about 10cm from the heat on one side for 3 minutes, brush the top side with more oil and turn over for another 2 minutes or until the skin is crisp
5. serve immediately

Notes: 1. if you have to prepare the sardines it is quite easy. Hold a sardine in one hand and snap off the head pulling downwards. Most of the guts should come off with the head. Cut down the belly with a sharp knife and use a finger to remove the rest of the guts. You can then remove the backbone by pulling the top of it firmly, if necessary loosening it with a sharp knife. Rinse well inside and out and pat dry.

2. other fish suitable for grilling are red mullet, grey mullet, sea bream, sea bass if not too large and white fish steaks. If they have been scaled, gutted and cleaned you should make two diagonal slashes on each side with a sharp knife and proceed as above but because they are larger than they will take longer and if they are not done may need to be moved further away from the grill if the skin starts to crisp and blacken

(they are done when you can see through the slashes that the flesh is white right down to the bone).

# ROASTED SEA BASS STUFFED WITH FENNEL

Serves 4
Takes 20 minutes

## Ingredients

4 x 450g sea bass (loup de mer) scaled and gutted
2 tablespoons olive oil
Salt and pepper
A large bunch of fennel herb
4 tablespoons pastis (such as Pernod, Ricard or Ouzo)

## Method

1. pre-heat the oven to 220C /gas mark 7
2. rub each fish inside and out with olive oil and salt and pepper
3. stuff fennel into the cavity of each fish and add a teaspoon of pastis to it
4. oil a baking tin large enough to hold the fish and make a bed for it to rest on with the remaining fennel
5. rub more oil over the outside of the fish, place on the bed of fennel and sprinkle the rest of the pastis over the fish
6. put into the oven for 15 minutes
7. remove and serve immediately

# MOROCCAN FISH FILLETS

Spicy and delicious this is almost a fish curry
Serves 4
Takes about 1 hour 15 minutes

## Ingredients

4 x 200g fillets of cod or hake
20 waxy new potatoes
20 cherry tomatoes
4 large green peppers (or 2 green and 2 red if you prefer)
4 garlic cloves peeled and sliced
12 black olives
3 tablespoons olive oil
Salt and pepper
100ml water

## Marinade ingredients

2 garlic cloves peeled and sliced
1 teaspoon sea salt
2 teaspoons ground cumin
Juice of 1 lemon
2 tsp red wine vinegar
1 teaspoon mild paprika
1 small bunch coriander chopped
1 tablespoon olive oil
1 dessertspoon rose harissa (optional if you can't find it)

## Method

1. first make the marinade in a bowl or mortar. Grind the garlic into a paste with the salt then stir in the other ingredients.
2. pat the fish fillets dry with a paper towel, smear half the marinade over them and leave in the fridge while you get on with the rest of the preparation
3. cut the peppers into quarters and grill, skin side up, under a hot grill until blackened then remove the black burnt bits

4. peel the potatoes and boil in salted water for 10 minutes then drain and place them in a saucepan or frying pan large enough to take the fish in one layer. NB the pan must have a lid.
5. heat the 3 tbsp olive oil in a pan and fry the garlic until turning golden then add the tomatoes, peppers, olives and the remaining marinade and  heat through for 2 or 3 minutes, stirring then tip most of it over the potatoes, keeping back a little
6. place the fish on top and drizzle over the remaining marinade
7. pour in the water, cover with the lid and place on a high heat. Keep the water boiling so the fish is steamed. After 10 minutes take a peek to see if the fish is cooked. It should be pearly with the flakes just coming apart.

# CHICKEN FAJITAS
South of the border down Mexico way
Serves 4
Takes about 30 minutes

## Ingredients
3 tablespoons olive oil
2 boneless chicken breasts cut into thin strips
1 medium onion halved and then sliced
2 cloves garlic thinly sliced
2 red peppers, de-seeded and cut into thin slices
1 courgette, ends cut off and sliced into thin strips
8 flour tortillas
150 ml sour cream
1 small tub of ready-made guacamole or 1 avocado cut into strips
1 small bunch of spring onions trimmed and thinly sliced
## Method
1. put the guacamole or avocado slices, sour cream and spring onions into bowls
2. put the tortillas into a slow oven to keep warm
3. heat the oil and fry the onions, pepper, courgette and garlic over a low-medium heat for about 5 minutes until softened,
4. increase the heat, add the chicken and continue to cook stirring constantly until the vegetables have a slightly blackened look around the edges and the chicken is cooked
5. serve immediately with the other ingredients passed separately so everyone can make their own fajitas

If wished a bowl of chopped fresh tomatoes, skinned and de-seeded is a pleasant addition.

# LAMB CURRY

If the boys are really missing their curry this is quick and easy
Serves 4
Takes about 50 minutes

## Ingredients

4 tablespoons olive oil
400g lamb cubed
2 medium onions halved and then sliced
4 cloves garlic thinly sliced
1 litre beef stock
2 heaped dessertspoons medium curry powder
A handful of sultanas
2 tablespoons dessicated coconut
Basmati rice
250 ml Greek style yoghurt

## Method

1. heat the olive oil in a large pan and fry the lamb over a medium/high heat with the curry powder.
2. turn the heat down and add the sliced onion and garlic when the lamb is browned (about 5 minutes) and stir around. The longer you cook at this stage the more mellow the curry will be.
3. throw in the sultanas and dessicated coconut and pour in the stock
4. give a good stir, turn up the heat to bring to the boil and then lower the heat and simmer for 30 minutes or so while the sauce thickens
5. cook the rice according to the packet instructions

Serve with the rice, yoghurt, a jar of mango chutney and perhaps some sliced banana.

# PORK SPARE RIBS

Serves 4
Takes 60 minutes

## Ingredients
2 tablespoons olive oil
1.25 kg pork spare ribs

### Sauce ingredients
100 ml dry sherry
2 cloves garlic thinly sliced
5 tsp smoked Spanish paprika (pimenton)
1 tablespoon oregano
150 ml water
1 tsp salt

## Method
1. preheat the oven to 220 degrees centigrade
2. oil a large roasting tin and place the spare ribs in a single layer then roast in the oven for 20 minutes
3. put the sauce ingredients into a jar and shake vigorously
4. when the spare ribs have roasted for 20 minutes remove from the oven and turn the heat down to 180 degrees Centigrade
5. pour the sauce over the ribs and turn to ensure that they are all coated then return to the oven for a further 40 minutes, basting with the sauce 2 or 3 times
6. when the ribs are done, remove them and keep them warm.
7. place the roasting tin on the hob and bring to the boil then turn down the heat slightly and reduce the sauce to about half.
8. pour over the ribs and serve with plenty of kitchen towel.

## 1. CHEATING

One of the best dodges is to buy a "Poulet Roti" which are widely available in France, often sold at the roadside and are whole chickens roasted on a revolving spit and can be taken away in insulated foil bags to keep them warm. It may be necessary to pre-order them.
They are sometimes supplied with frites.

Keep your eyes open..

## VEGETABLES TO GO WITH  MAIN MEALS

| RECIPE | PAGE |
|---|---|
| Lemony potatoes | 73 |
| Grilled  asparagus | 74 |
| Braised fennel | 75 |
| Courgettes with tomatoes and garlic | 76 |
| Green beans | 77 |
| Grilled potatoes | 78 |
| Potato salad with lardons and capers | 79 |
| Spinach | 80 |

# LEMONY POTATOES

Serves 4
Takes 30 minutes

**Ingredients**
600g small potatoes, cut in half if necessary so they are of the same size
½ a lemon
1 clove garlic finely chopped
2 tablespoons olive oil
Salt and pepper
1 tablespoon capers

**Method**
1. pre-heat the oven to 190C/gas mark 6
2. remove the zest from the lemon with a grater or if you don't have one use a potato peeler or sharp knife and cut into tiny pieces, squeeze the juice of the lemon into a bowl and add the garlic and oil. Stir well.
3. toss the potatoes in the liquid in the bowl, arrange in a roasting tin and sprinkle over salt and pepper and the lemon zest
4. cook in the centre of the oven for 30 minutes turning once or twice
5. scatter over the capers and cook for a further 5 minutes

# GRILLED ASPARAGUS

Serves 4

Takes 10 minutes

**Ingredients**

24 asparagus spears

½ a lemon

2 tablespoons olive oil

Salt and pepper

**Method**

1. heat the grill or griddle pan if using
2. put the aspargus in a large bowl, pour over the olive oil and use your hands to ensure that all the spears have a coating of oil
3. place on the grill and cook, turning once until you have some lightly charred bands/patches and the asparagus is softened (about 7-10 minutes)
4. sprinkle with salt and pepper and lemon juice

# BRAISED FENNEL

Serves 4
Takes 1 hour

**Ingredients**
4 fennel bulbs
2 garlic cloves crushed
3 tablespoons olive oil
1 can tomato pieces
Salt and pepper

**Method**

1. heat the oil in a large saucepan or frying pan with a lid on a medium heat
2. remove the outer fennel leaves if very coarse or discoloured, trim off the base and cut in half lengthways
3. add the fennel and garlic to the pan, season with salt and pepper and turn in the oil to get a coating.
4. cover and stew for 30 minutes, turning occasionally
5. drain the tomato pieces in a sieve and add them to the pan.
6. cook for another 20 minutes or so. Taste for seasoning and serve.

# COURGETTES WITH TOMATOES

Serves 4

Takes 30 minutes plus 1 hour for salting the courgettes

**Ingredients**
   4 medium courgettes
   4 tomatoes skinned and roughly chopped
   1 clove garlic finely chopped
   2 tablespoons olive oil
   Salt and pepper

**Method**
1. slice the courgettes into rounds a bit less than 1cm thick
2. place in a colander and sprinkle with salt. Leave for an hour. Rinse with water and pat dry
3. heat the oil in a saucepan and when hot add the courgettes and then the garlic
4. cook the courgettes over a medium heat, moving about and turning over as they colour
5. when the courgettes have softened add the tomatoes and when they have reduced and thickened, season with salt and pepper.
6. can be served hot or cold.

# GREEN BEANS

Serves 4
Takes 10 minutes

## Ingredients
300 grams French beans
Salt

## Method

1. bring a large pan of salted water to the boil
2. meanwhile cut the stalks off the beans
3. put the beans in the water and boil for 4 minutes then spear one with a fork and take a small bite to see if they are ready. If not give them longer and apply the bite check at intervals.
4. when ready drain, and if they are to be eaten cold as part of a salad refresh under the cold water tap.

# GRILLED POTATOES

Delicious with grilled fish or steak. I like them better than chips.
Serves 4
Takes 20 minutes

## Ingredients
2 large firm potatoes such as Desiree
3 tablespoons olive oil
dried Herbes de Provence
Salt

## Method

1. bring a large pan of salted water to the boil
2. meanwhile peel the potatoes and cut into slices about 1 cm thick
3. cook the potatoes in the water until just cooked (test with the point of a knife)
4. heat the grill or barbeque
5. drain the potatoes and brush with olive oil then place on the grill pan and sprinkle with a little pinch of herbes de provence and a little salt
6. grill until a little golden then turn and do the other side.

# POTATO SALAD WITH LARDONS AND CAPERS

Serves 4
Takes 30 minutes

## Ingredients
600 grams medium/large potatoes, peeled if necessary and cut into 2cm chunks
1 tablespoon capers rinsed under the tap in a sieve
100 grams streaky bacon cut into small pieces or lardons
4 tablespoons olive oil
2 tablespoons red wine vinegar
1 teaspoon dried thyme
Salt and pepper

## Method
1. boil the potato pieces in salted water until cooked but firm
2. meanwhile heat a tablespoon of olive oil in a frying pan and fry the bacon until crisp.
3. drain the potatoes and while still warm add the capers and toss in 3 tablespoons olive oil. Season with salt and pepper.
4. add the red wine vinegar to the lardons in the frying pan and let it thicken (only takes a minute or two).
5. pour the lardons and reduced vinegar over the potatoes and stir
6. sprinkle with dried thyme and serve.

# SPINACH

This goes really well with grilled fish

Serves 4
Takes 10 minutes

## Ingredients
   500 grams young spinach leaves
   1 tablespoon butter
   1 tablespoon olive oil
   1 level teaspoon grated nutmeg
   Salt and pepper

## Method

1. wash the spinach and then shake in a colander to remove as much of the water as you can
2. melt the butter and olive oil in a large pan on a medium-high heat
3. throw in the spinach leaves stirring with a wooden spoon so they wilt
4. sprinkle over the nutmeg, salt and pepper and stir letting the moisture evaporate
5. serve when the right consistency is reached.

# CHEESE

I am definitely with the continentals when it comes to having the cheese course before the dessert – just the thing to finish the wine with – c'est logique! And with so many wonderful cheeses to choose from I can hover for hours at the cheese counter or better still a market stall.

# DESSERTS

I'm afraid I'm not into making puddings on holiday when there are so many fruit tarts, gateaux and other delights to be bought, expertly made, in patisseries and wonderful fresh fruit, fragrant ripe peaches and apricots which never taste the same when bought at home. So on holiday my family generally have to make do with those things and ice-cream.

However in case puddings are your passion then here are a few favourite recipes.

| RECIPE | PAGE |
|---|---|
| Normandy Apple Tart | 83 |
| Little pots of Chocolate | 85 |
| Lemon pudding | 87 |
| Baked apricots | 88 |
| Bananas with rum and cream | 89 |
| Caramelised oranges | 90 |

# NORMANDY APPLE TART

A real French classic. This version follows Elizabeth David's methods, especially for making foolproof pastry with no nonsense about rolling pins or chilling in the fridge.

Serves 6
Takes 50 minutes
You will need a flan tin about 20 centimeters (8 inches) in diameter
**Ingredients**

**Filling:**
1 kilo of sweet dessert apples peeled, cored and thinly sliced
75 grams butter
4 tablespoons of caster sugar

**Pastry:**
100 grams of butter at room temperature
200 grams of plain flour
A quarter teaspoon of salt
3 teaspoons of caster sugar
A glass of water with ice cubes floating in it

**Method**
Preheat the oven to 200 degrees centigrade with a metal baking sheet in the oven.
Lightly butter the flan tin.

For the filling:
1. melt the butter in a large frying pan, add the apples and sprinkle over the sugar.
2. cook very gently until the apples are golden and becoming transparent. Try not to let the pieces break up so if you have to stir them be gentle with them
3. take the apples off the heat when they are cooked and allow to cool

4. while the apples are cooking make the pastry

For the pastry
1. sieve the flour into a large bowl
2. add the salt and sugar and stir
3. take pieces of butter and rub them with your fingertips into the flour until the whole is used up and the mixture is like coarse breadcrumbs
4. sprinkle with 2 tablespoons of ice water and shape into a ball. If you need to add more water do it a half spoonful at a time but use as little as possible
5. put the ball of pastry into the flan tin and flatten it with your hand
6. use your fingers and knuckles to spread the pastry over the flan tin and up the sides patching up any gaps and keeping the pastry as thin as possible
7. prick all over with a fork including each ridge in the sides
8. carefully arrange the apple pieces in an overlapping circle starting at the outside and working inwards
9. brush the exposed edges of the pastry with milk
10. place the tin on the baking sheet in the oven and cook for 30 minutes. Check after 15 minutes and if one side of the pastry is cooking more than the other turn the tin through 180 degrees.
11. after 30 minutes reheat the buttery juices in which the apples were cooked and pour them over the apples in the tart.
12. cook for a minute or two longer until the pastry is nicely golden
13. serve with some crème fraiche or vanilla ice cream if desired. Can be served hot or cold.

# LITTLE POTS OF CHOCOLATE

Especially for chocoholics! Really rich so a little goes a long way..

Serves 4
Takes 30 minutes plus 45 minutes cooking plus several hours in the fridge so you need to plan ahead, but it is really easy.
You will need a 2 inch deep baking tin and 4 little pots (or use coffee cups if you don't have any)

**Ingredients**
175ml double cream
½ a vanilla pod split open lengthways
125 grams of dark bitter chocolate
75 ml of milk
1 tablespoon of icing sugar
2 small egg yolks

**Method**
1. Place a baking tin half filled with water (i.e. about 1 inch of water) in the oven.
2. Preheat the oven to 160 degrees centigrade.
3. Warm (but don't boil) the cream with the vanilla pod in a saucepan then cover and leave for 30 minutes
4. while the cream is infusing:
  1.break the chocolate into bits and gently melt in the milk in a separate saucepan stirring occasionally
  2. separate the egg yolks, discard the whites and beat the yolks with the icing sugar in a large bowl
5. when the cream has had 30 minutes to infuse, fish out and discard the vanilla pod then blend the cream with the egg yolks in the bowl and then blend the chocolate into the mixture whisking thoroughly until all the little bits of chocolate have disappeared
6. press the mixture through a fine mesh sieve into a clean bowl and then spoon the sieved mixture into the little pots so it comes about 2/3rds of the way up

7. place in the heated water in the baking tin and cook for 45 minutes or until the mixture has risen slightly and a crust has formed which may take another 15 minutes or so
8. remove and allow to cool then place in the fridge for at least 4 hours

# LEMON PUDDING

This separates into a spongy top with a thick runny sauce underneath.
Yummy!

Serves 4
Takes 15 minutes plus 40 minutes cooking
You will need a deep baking tin and a souffle dish

## Ingredients
  50 grams of butter
  150 grams of caster sugar
  1 large lemon
  50 grams plain flour
  250 ml milk
  2 eggs

## Method
1. Place a baking tin half filled with water (i.e. about 1 inch of water) in the oven.
2. Preheat the oven to 200 degrees centigrade.
3. separate the eggs and beat the yolks
4. in a large bowl cream together the butter and sugar until light and fluffy
5. grate the zest off the lemon and add to the bowl and then squeeze the lemon and add the juice
6. mix in the flour, the milk and then beat in the beaten egg yolks
7. in a separate bowl beat the egg whites until they stand up in stiff peaks
8. butter the soufflé dish
9. fold the beaten egg whites into the other ingredients and pour the mixture into the souffle dish
10. stand the soufflé dish in the water in the baking tin in the oven and cook for 30-40 minutes until golden

# BAKED APRICOTS

Serves 4
Takes 10 minutes plus 15 minutes cooking
You will need an ovenproof dish

## Ingredients
Butter, for greasing the dish
4 apricots
4 tbsp flaked almonds
4 tbsp runny honey
¼ teaspoon ground nutmeg

## Method
1. Pre-heat the oven to 200 degrees centigrade
2. lightly butter the dish
3. cut each apricot in half and remove the stone
4. arrange the apricot halves in the dish, skin side down and drizzle the honey over them then sprinkle with the almonds and the nutmeg.
5. bake in the oven for 15 minutes
6. serve with vanilla ice-cream if desired.

# BANANAS WITH RUM AND CREAM

Very easy and involves no cooking. Young children enjoy making this.

Serves 4
Takes 10 minutes maximum

## Ingredients
    4 bananas
    1 tablespoon soft dark brown sugar
    200 ml thick double cream
    2 tablespoons dark rum

### Method
1. stir the cream and rum together in a large bowl
2. slice the bananas into rounds and add to the cream
3. stir and divide between 4 bowls
4. sprinkle with the sugar and serve

# CARAMELISED ORANGES

Serves 4
Takes 20 minutes plus 1 hour chilling time

## Ingredients
4 oranges
250 grams caster sugar
300 ml water

## Method
1. pare the zest of 2 of the oranges off with a sharp knife or potato peeler then cut the pared zest into thin strips – as thin as you can get them
2. peel all the oranges, removing all the white pith
3. cut the oranges into thin slices preserving the juice
4. put the sugar and 150 ml of the water in a saucepan over a medium heat stirring until the water boils and the sugar dissolves then boil without stirring until the syrup turns golden brown
5. off the heat add the rest of the water and the strips of zest, return to the heat and stir until the caramel is fully merged with the water.
6. allow to cool a little then pour over the oranges, stir gently to mix the juice into the syrup
7. put into a shallow bowl and spread out the orange slices.
8. cover with cling-film and leave in the fridge until cold

# DRINKS

| RECIPE | PAGE |
|---|---|
| Sangria | 92 |
| Fizz | 93 |
| Lemonade | 94 |

# SANGRIA

Goes well with the sun and sand….
Makes 6 glasses
Takes 10 minutes


**Ingredients**
2 oranges sliced, slices cut in half
2 lemons sliced, slices cut in half
50 ml brandy
1 bottle of red wine chilled
100 grams caster sugar
Ice cubes

**Method**
1. put the brandy and fruit into a large jug and stir with a spoon squashing the fruit to release the juice
2. add the wine and the sugar and stir until dissolved
3. chill in the fridge until needed than add ice cubes before serving

# FUN WITH FIZZ

Prosecco in Italy, Cava in Spain and of course Champagne in France all are delicious and chic on their own, however for a little variety there are variations:

## Buck's Fizz
Mix with chilled orange juice (freshly squeezed for preference – it's worth the effort).

## Kir Royale
Put a little Liqueur de Cassis or Framboise in the glass before adding the champagne. The proportions are a matter of taste and it's fun finding out what suits you.

## Champagne Cooler
Half fill a tall glass with ice, add a dessertspoon each of brandy and Cointreau. Top up with champagne.  Stir and garnish with mint.

## Bellini
Mix 1 part of chilled peach juice with 3 parts champagne. I like to substitute apricot juice for the peach juice.

# LEMONADE

Makes 4 glasses
Takes 5 minutes

## Ingredients
8 lemons
200 grams caster sugar
700 ml water

## Method
1. boil the water
2. grate the zest of the lemons into a heat-proof bowl then squeeze the juice into the bowl as well.
3. add the sugar, pour on the boiling water and stir until the sugar is dissolved
4. allow to cool then chill in the fridge
5. when ready to use dilute with cold water and add more sugar according to your taste.

# DRESSINGS

## MAYONNAISE

Once you have made this glossy yellow mayonnaise you may never want to buy the pre-prepared jars again. Wonderful with cold asparagus or freshly cooked prawns.

Makes 150ml
Takes 10 minutes

**Ingredients**
1 egg yolk
1 teaspoon Dijon mustard
½ teaspoon salt
¼ teaspoon pepper
1 tablespoon lemon juice
150ml extra virgin olive oil (must be good quality)

**Method**
1. put the egg yolk in a bowl with the salt and pepper and one teaspoon of the lemon juice
2. add the oil drop by drop to begin with and then in a thin stream, whisking all the time until the sauce is thick and smooth. If it becomes too thick add a little more lemon juice
3. when all the oil is in gradually stir in the remaining lemon juice
4. will keep for up to 3 days in a screw top jar in the fridge


## VINAIGRETTE

Makes 200ml
Takes 5 minutes

**Ingredients**
175ml extra virgin olive oil
35ml red wine vinegar
1 teaspoon runny honey or sugar
1 teaspoon Dijon mustard

¼ teaspoon salt
½ teaspoon pepper

**Method**
1. Place all the ingredients in a screw top jar and shake vigorously to emulsify
2. taste (I use a finger but don't tell anyone) and add more salt and pepper if wished.

Notes: if liked add a crushed garlic clove or some finely chopped fresh herbs such as tarragon, parsley or marjoram at step 1

## BALSAMIC VINEGAR DRESSING

**Ingredients**
1 tablespoon good quality aged balsamic vinegar (don't get cheap stuff it tastes too raw)
3 tablespoons extra virgin olive oil
Salt and pepper

**Method**
1. Place all the ingredients in a screw top jar and shake vigorously to emulsify
2. taste and adjust according to your taste.

## TABLE OF EQUIVALENT OVEN TEMPERATURES

Careful when self-catering, oven temperatures of a strange oven can vary a lot from your oven at home, particularly if you are used to a fan oven.

|  | Fahrenheit | Centigrade | Gas |
|---|---|---|---|
| Slow | 240-510 | 115-155 | ¼-2 |
| Moderate | 320-370 | 160-190 | 3-4 |
| Fairly hot | 380-400 | 195-205 | 5 |
| Hot | 410-440 | 210-230 | 6-7 |
| Very hot | 450-480 | 235-250 | 8-9 |

## APPROXIMATE EQUIVALENT WEIGHTS

| METRIC | ENGLISH |
|---|---|
| 1 Kilogram = 1000 grams | 2lb 3 oz |
| 500 grams | 1lb 1 oz |
| 250 grams | 9oz |
| 100 grams | 3.5oz |

# INDEX

Pilaff, lamb 51
Pizza 29
Pork Spare Ribs 70
Pork, with sage and
capers 53
Potatoes, grilled 78
Potatoes, lemony 73
Potato salad 79
Poulet Roti 71
Prawns in Garlic 42
Prawns with chorizo
and rice 27

Salads:
  Courgette 26
  Couscous 17
  Crudites 41
  Enthusiastic 14-15
  Frisee au lardons 41
  Greek 28
  Goats Cheese 39
  Nicoise 19
  Tomato & Bread 16
  Tricolore 42
  Tsatsiki 38
Sangria 92
Sardines, grilled 63
Sea Bass, roasted 65
Spaghetti alla
Pomodori 44
Spaghetti alla
Putanesca 45
Spanish Omelette 32
Spinach 80
Steak 57

Tagine, Lamb 49
Tomato and bread
salad 16
Tortilla 32-33

Vegetables:
Asparagus, cold 41
Asparagus, grilled 74
Beans, green 77
Courgettes with
tomatoes 76
Fennel, braised 75
Potatoes, grilled 78
Potatoes, lemony 73
Potato salad 79
Spinach 80
Vinaigrette 95

**About the author**
Tony Nelson has enjoyed self-catering family holidays for years and his lovingly assembled collection of tried and tested (on his family), recipes and practical tips are all included in this book.
He has had a lot of fun with holiday cookery and wants to share it with others and help to make the world a happier and more contented, place.